Spe

Functional English: writing

Emma Darley and Helen Darley

Acknowledgements

© 2008 Folens Limited, on behalf of the author.

United Kingdom: Folens Publishers, Waterslade House, Thame Road, Haddenham, Buckinghamshire, HP17 8NT.
Email: folens@folens.com

Ireland: Folens Publishers, Greenhills Road, Tallaght, Dublin 24.
Email: info@folens.ie

Editor: Cathy Hurren

Cover design: Samantha Dilley

Illustrations: Katy Dynes

Layout artist: Planman Technologies

Cover image: © iStockphoto.com/livjam

First published 2008 by Folens Limited.

Every effort has been made to contact copyright holders of material used in this publication. If any copyright holder has been overlooked, we should be pleased to make any necessary arrangements.

British Library Cataloguing in Publication Data. A catalogue record for this publication is available from the British Library.

ISBN 978-1-85008-382-5

Contents

Introduction

Specials! *English* has been specifically written for teachers to use with students who may struggle with some of the skills and concepts needed for Key Stage 3 English. The titles are part of a wider series from Folens for use with lower ability students.

Each book in the series contains ten separate units covering the topics needed to complete the theme of the book. Each unit has one or more photocopiable Resource sheets and several Activity sheets. This allows the teacher to work in different ways. The tasks are differentiated throughout the book and offer all students the opportunity to expand their skills.

The Teacher's notes give guidance and are laid out as follows:

Objectives
These are the main skills or knowledge to be learned.

Prior knowledge
This refers to the minimum skills or knowledge required by the students to complete the tasks. As a rule, students should have a reading comprehension age of six to nine years and should be working at levels 1 to 3. Some Activity sheets are more challenging than others and will need to be selected accordingly.

NC links
All units link to aspects of the English Framework at Key Stage 3, the National Curriculum for English, the National Curriculum in Wales, Scottish attainment targets and the Northern Ireland PoS.

Background
This provides additional information related to writing skills.

Starter activity
Since the units can be taught as a lesson, a warm-up activity focusing on an aspect of the unit is suggested.

Resource sheets and Activity sheets
The Resource sheets contain no tasks and can be used as a stimulus for discussion. Related tasks are provided on the Activity sheets.

Plenary
The teacher can use the suggestions here to do additional work, recap on the main points covered, or reinforce a particular point.

Assessment sheet
At the end of the book is an Assessment sheet focusing on student progress. It can be used in different ways. A student could complete it as a self-assessment, while the teacher also completes one on the student's progress. The two can then be compared. This is useful in situations where the teacher or classroom assistant is working with one student. Alternatively, students could work in pairs to carry out peer assessments and then compare the outcomes with each other.

Starting from a simple base that students can manage, the Assessment sheet allows them to discuss their own progress, consider different points of view, discuss how they might improve and allow the teacher to see the work from the student's perspective.

Teacher's notes

Using short, simple sentences

Objectives

- To use well-constructed, grammatically correct simple sentences
- To understand subjects and verbs within a sentence

Prior knowledge

It would be useful for students to have knowledge of verbs and capital letters.

English Framework links

Yr7 Sentence 3, 6; Yr8 Sentence 2

Scottish attainment targets

English Language – Writing
Strand – Knowledge about language: Levels B, C, D, E

National Curriculum in Wales links

Writing: 3; Language development 1, 2

Northern Ireland PoS

Language and literacy: developing their knowledge of how language works.

Background

When trying to improve students' grammatical constructions, a useful starting place is to look at simple sentences. Once students have understood the components (for example, a subject and verb in a simple sentence) they will then be able to build upon this knowledge and look at other sentence constructions, such as compound or complex sentences. However, before moving on, establishing the basics is important and this section allows you to introduce these grammatical concepts in a straightforward, easy way.

Teaching the fundamental rules behind sentences can vastly improve a student's writing. It can ensure that punctuation is used and that sentences make sense. It should also make students much more confident writers.

Starter activity

To assess students' knowledge of sentences, it would be a good idea to ask them how they would answer the question: what is a sentence? Try to encourage answers such as: a group of words, a string of words, a chain of words, something which ends with a piece of punctuation, and so on.

Resource sheets and Activity sheets

The Activity sheet, 'What are simple sentences?', breaks down simple sentences into four rules. Students have the opportunity to look at a list of examples and, based upon the four rules, decide whether these are simple sentences or not. This activity will particularly focus their attention on the fact that a simple sentence must contain a verb and end with a piece of punctuation.

Once students have an overall understanding of this sentence type, they could then expand their knowledge of how verbs work within a simple sentence. The Activity sheet, 'Identifying the verb', will show students that to create a grammatically correct sentence, there must be a verb present.

Once students have identified the fact that a clause contains a verb, they could then be introduced to the concept of a subject. By breaking a sentence down into its components (the subject and the verb), students will understand how a sentence is formed. The Activity sheet, 'Identifying the subject', helps to introduce this concept to students and the Activity sheet, 'Spotting verbs and subjects', then provides students with a chance to revise both of these components.

Finally, once students are confident with the grammatical components of these sentences, they could attempt to write their own using the Activity sheet, 'Writing your own simple sentences'. This provides students with a picture to help inspire six of their own sentences.

Plenary

To end the lesson, it would be a good idea to refer back to the students' initial definition of a sentence from the Starter activity. Ask the students if they would like to make any amendments to this; hopefully they will insert a reference to a verb and a subject (if these were not initially referred to).

Activity sheet – Using short, simple sentences

What are simple sentences?

A simple sentence is a group of words (a clause). There are four rules to remember when writing a simple sentence:

1   It must make sense on its own.

2   It must always start with a capital letter.

3   It must contain a verb (a doing word).

4   It must end with a piece of punctuation such as a full stop, exclamation mark or question mark. It cannot end with a comma.

☞   Read the sentences in the table below. Decide if they are simple sentences or not and put a tick or a cross in the appropriate column. The first one has been done for you.

	✓	✗
I am very happy today.	✓	
Hello!		
the shop was never		
Even though,		
Will you be going again?		
A big, scary house.		
My favourite food is chocolate.		
Why?		
Why don't you finish that?		
Goodbye!		
Help!		
I went shopping.		
The dog licked the bowl.		
hopefully not		
Last night I watched television.		
He always plays football.		

Identifying the verb

Remember, simple sentences must use a verb (a doing word).

☞ Read the following simple sentences and circle all of the verbs that are used. The first one has been done for you.

- The boy (went) to the beach.

- The boy was sweating.

- The boy bought an ice cream from the shop.

- The boy quickly ate his ice cream.

- The ice cream melted.

- The boy threw away the last bit of his ice cream.

- The boy wiped his sticky fingers.

- The boy needed a drink.

- The boy took out a bottle from his bag.

- The boy drank his drink.

- The boy decided to lie down on the sand.

- The boy could hear the waves.

- The boy fell asleep.

- The sun was shining.

Activity sheet – Using short, simple sentences

Identifying the subject

As well as having a verb, a simple sentence must also have a subject – this is the person or thing that performs the action.

 Read the following sentences and circle the subject within each one. The first one has been done for you.

- The (dog) entered the lounge.

- The mum ran after the dog with a cloth.

- The boy laughed.

- The mum wiped the carpet.

- The dog escaped into the garden.

- The boy stopped laughing.

- The dog liked to play in the garden.

- The dog started to eat the plants.

- The mum banged on the window.

- The girl was trying to sleep on the sofa.

- The girl woke up.

- The mum apologised.

- The dog lay down on the lawn.

- The boy turned on the television.

Activity sheet – Using short, simple sentences

Spotting verbs and subjects

Now that you know a little bit more about simple sentences, you could attempt the exercise below.

☞ Complete the following table by identifying both the subject and the verb in each of the sentences. The first two have been done for you.

Simple sentences	Subject	Verb
Some students study at school.	students	study
John plays football at school.	John	plays
Sarah goes to the library.		
The teachers eat in the staffroom.		
The students eat in the canteen.		
The caretaker walks around the grounds.		
The head teacher drives a fast car.		
The secretary works in her office.		
The class dislike their teacher.		
The teachers like to give homework.		
The students play games at break time.		
The building is starting to crumble.		

Activity sheet – Using short, simple sentences

Writing your own simple sentences

☞ Using the picture as inspiration, try to write six simple sentences of your own in the spaces provided.

Remember, each one must:

- have a capital letter at the start
- end with a piece of punctuation such as a full stop, exclamation mark or question mark
- include a subject
- include a verb
- make sense on its own.

1 _____

_____

_____

2 _____

_____

_____

3 _____

_____

_____

4 _____

_____

_____

5 _____

_____

_____

6 _____

_____

_____

Functional English: writing

Teacher's notes

Using upper and lower case letters

Objectives

- To understand when to use upper and lower case letters
- To understand why we use upper and lower case letters

Prior knowledge

It would be helpful for students to have a basic understanding of capital letters.

English Framework links

Yr7 Sentence 17; Yr8 Sentence 8; Yr9 Sentence 9

Scottish attainment targets

English Language – Writing
Strand – Knowledge about language: Level B

National Curriculum in Wales links

Writing: 3; Language development 4

Northern Ireland PoS

Language and literacy: developing their knowledge of how language works.

Background

Teachers are constantly correcting capital letters within students' work, despite the fact that it was probably one of the first rules of grammar that they learned in school. It is sometimes apparent that students have forgotten the less common rules of capital letters, such as a person's title, or they simply forget to check back through their work. Either way, it is essential that, as students write each word, they should be able to justify their reasons for using either upper or lower case letters; this way, mistakes can be prevented.

Starter activity

A useful activity would be to ascertain how much the students already know about using upper and lower case letters. They could be asked the question: when should capital letters be used within writing? Their answers could be recorded, but not discussed at this point, as this will be referred back to throughout the following activities.

Resource sheets and Activity sheets

The first activity students could attempt is on the Activity sheet, 'Correcting upper and lower case letters'. This task allows students to look at a piece of writing in context and circle any incorrect upper and lower case letters. When discussing the answers with the students, it is important to ask them to justify why they have circled certain errors: they should give reasons, such as capitals are needed for the start of a person's name.

So that students can explain the rules of capitals, the following activities look at individual rules for using them. The Activity sheet, 'Capital places and capital letters', teaches students that all country and place names need a capital letter.

The Activity sheet, 'Famous marriages', then teaches students that people's names are always given capital letters. The answers to this activity are: 1b; 2a; 3h; 4g; 5d; 6e; 7c; 8f.

Students often make errors with people's titles, therefore the Activity sheet, 'Capital letters for titles', revises the rules for titles, concentrating on an extract about the Royal Family.

Finally, to consolidate students' knowledge, the Activity sheet, 'Revising your knowledge', tests all of the rules covered in this section and ensures that students always justify their use of capital letters within their writing.

Plenary

The students could now be referred back to the Starter activity and their initial answers about when to use capital letters. Ask them if they can add any more rules to their answers.

Activity sheet – Using upper and lower case letters

Correcting upper and lower case letters

☞ Have a look at the letter below. Some of the upper and lower case letters have been typed incorrectly. Pretend you are a teacher marking this work and circle all of the letters that are wrong with a red pen.

dear mr briggs

I am writing to inform you about the dreadful Behaviour of your son, raYmond. Recently, he has performed several practical jokes and stunts which this school will not tolerate and I urge you to speak to your son and reMind him of the seriousness of his actions.

On a recent trip to london he thought it would be funny to see whether his school coat would float in the River Thames. when he discovered that it would, he then started taking bets as to what other garments would float. he then stripped off, down to his underwear, and threw his other clothes into the water. This is comPletely unacceptable behaviour.

Secondly, raymond, who is constantly late for lessons, enlisted the help of his friends during lunchtime and set about turning all of the school clocks back by one hour. Had it not been for the quick action of our caretaker, mr myers, raymond could have suffered a serious injury when he attempted to climb up to the clock on the front of the school building.

I am sure that you will agree, such Behaviour is completely unacceptable and will not be tolerated.

I look forward to hearing your response to this matter.

Yours sincerely,

Mr jenson
Head Teacher

Activity sheet – Using upper and lower case letters

Capital places and capital letters

You should always use a capital letter when you write the name of a place or the name of a country because they are proper nouns.

☞ Read the sentences below. Some of the place names and country names have not been given a capital letter. In the right-hand column, write in the correct word that should be used. The first one has been done for you.

Place names	Amended place names
The capital of austria is Vienna.	Austria
The capital of England is london.	
The capital of belgium is Brussels.	
The capital of cuba is Havana.	
The capital of sweden is Stockholm.	
The capital of the United States of America is washington DC.	
The capital of barbados is Bridgetown.	
The capital of egypt is cairo.	
The capital of Switzerland is bern.	
The capital of spain is madrid.	

Activity sheet – Using upper and lower case letters

Famous marriages

☞ 1 Match up the following famous couples by drawing a line between them. The first
   one has been done for you.

1	**The Queen is married to…**	a	…Victoria beckham.
2	**David Beckham is married to…**	b	…prince Philip, duke of Edinburgh.
3	**Sharon Osbourne is married to…**	c	…Cheryl cole.
4	**Sports presenter Gabby Logan is married to…**	d	…Peter andre.
5	**Katie Price is married to…**	e	…Louise Rednapp.
6	**jamie rednapp is married to…**	f	…Charles the Prince of wales.
7	**Ashley cole is married to…**	g	…rugby player, Kenny Logan.
8	**Diana the Princess of Wales was married to…**	h	…Ozzy osbourne.

☞ 2 Now reread each sentence and draw a circle around the letters that should be in
   capitals.

Activity sheet – Using upper and lower case letters

Capital letters for titles

Capital letters are also used for people's titles. For example:

- The Prime Minister
- The Princess Royal
- The Queen
- Her Royal Highness
- The King

☞ Read the following extract about the Queen and circle all of the letters that should be in capitals. (**Hint:** there are a total of 27 letters to change!)

---

queen elizabeth came to the throne in 1952 after the death of her father, king george VI.

The queen is married to prince philip, the duke of edinburgh. The royal family's surname is windsor.

They have many official residences such as: buckingham palace, windsor castle, balmoral castle and sandringham house.

The queen has had four children: prince charles, princess anne, prince Andrew and prince Edward.

Activity sheet – Using upper and lower case letters

Revising your knowledge

☞ Read the sentences in the table below and try to work out why each of the underlined letters are capital letters. Write the correct reason in the right-hand column. Choose reasons from the following list to help you:

- place name
- a title
- someone's name
- days of the week

The first one has been done for you.

Sentence	Reason
1 **L**iverpool is a city in the North-West of England.	*Place name*
2 Camilla Parker Bowles is married to **P**rince **C**harles.	
3 **S**pain is a great place to go on holiday.	
4 **L**ucy went to the cinema.	
5 On **M**onday we will be going swimming.	
6 When I'm old enough, I would like to study at **C**ardiff **U**niversity.	
7 She was called **M**rs Jenny Harding.	
8 Maybe we should meet on **S**aturday?	
9 The boy went to watch his favourite team at **O**ld **T**rafford.	
10 The **S**ergeant **M**ajor was injured in battle.	

Teacher's notes

Capital letters and full stops

Objectives

- To understand why sentences need a capital letter and a full stop

Prior knowledge

It would be useful for students to have some knowledge of simple sentences.

English Framework links

Yr7 Sentence 3; Yr8 Sentence 8; Yr9 Sentence 2

Scottish attainment targets

English Language – Writing
Strand – Punctuation and structure: Levels A, B, C, D, E

National Curriculum in Wales links

Writing: 3; Language development 1

Northern Ireland PoS

Language and literacy: developing their knowledge of how language works.

Background

For students to be able to write a grammatically correct sentence, they need to understand the rules behind capital letters and full stops. For many students, confusion often occurs within their writing when they forget to use full stops. This section attempts to show students how chaotic writing can be when full stops are omitted. It is important that students completely understand the reasoning behind why full stops and capital letters are needed if they are going to use them correctly within their own writing.

Starter activity

To assess students' knowledge, it would be a good idea to ask them why they think capital letters are used after full stops.

Resource sheets and Activity sheets

It is important that students realise a sentence must open with a capital letter and close with a piece of punctuation such as a full stop, question mark or exclamation mark in order for it to be grammatically correct. Students need to understand that a sentence closing with a comma is not a complete sentence. The Activity sheet, 'Capital letters and full stops', highlights this.

Now that students understand the rules behind full stops and capital letters, they could start to explore the reasoning behind using full stops. The Activity sheet, 'Full stops', shows why writers need to use them in order to prevent confusion within their writing.

The Activity sheet, 'A full stop confusion', then provides students with a further exercise to help realise why full stops are needed. The answers to this exercise are provided on the Resource sheet, 'Film review'.

Plenary

Now that students have explored this topic in detail, they could be asked the same question from the Starter activity. Hopefully, their answers are now more detailed and accurate.

Capital letters and full stops

It is important to remember that all sentences must start with a capital letter and finish with a piece of punctuation, in this case, a full stop.

☞ Put a tick next to the following sentences which have been correctly written and a cross next to those that have not. The first one has been done for you.

Peter Kay is a comedian from Bolton	✗
when he was at school, he only achieved one GCSE	
He has been named one of the greatest funny men of all time.	
he is famous for his television show, *Phoenix Nights*	
He has appeared in the TV soap, *Coronation Street*	
he has also produced a song, which went to the top of the charts.	
he has appeared in musical theatre	
Before he was famous, he used to work in a cash and carry.	
He has also worked in a factory.	
he has toured the country with his stand-up comedy shows	
He has appeared in a television advert.	

Functional English: writing

Activity sheet – Capital letters and full stops

Full stops

Full stops are used at the end of a sentence to:

- signal the end of a sentence
- show a strong pause
- help writing make sense.

Without any full stops, large blocks of text would be very confusing.

However, full stops are *not* needed at the end of titles or subtitles.

☞ All of the full stops have been removed from the following news article. Using a red pen, insert full stops into the correct places. (**Hint:** there are eight full stops to insert!)

Comedian scoops two comedy gongs

The world's funniest man proved to be as funny as ever after he scooped two awards last night This time he won them at the Oscars of the comedy world

Voted by readers of *Popular Weekly*, he won the Funniest Man Alive and Readers' Vote categories at the British Comedy Awards He looked shocked when his name was read out but made a very funny speech once he had accepted his award

The smash hit American show, *Another Funny Sitcom*, was named Best International Comedy Show

The British television show, *We're Just As Funny As Friends*, won the Best British Comedy Show award So many cast members tried to get on stage to accept this award that their speech went on for ten minutes

For a full list of winners, see our special supplement in this week's edition of *Popular Weekly*

Activity sheet – Capital letters and full stops

A full stop confusion

Without any full stops, pieces of text can seem very confusing and hard to read.

☞ Read the following film review. The writer has forgotten to use any full stops. Insert the missing full stops and circle any letters that should be in capitals after the full stop.

Film Review
Shaun of the Dead

Released in 2004, *Shaun of the Dead* is a comedy film written by Simon Pegg and Edgar Wright both writers previously worked on the successful television show *Spaced Shaun of the Dead* has been successful in both the UK and America the film is about Shaun, a young man who has lots of relationship problems:  his girlfriend has just dumped him and he has arguments with his mum about his stepdad as well as Shaun's personal problems, it seems that London, and the rest of the world, is being taken over by zombies however, part of the comedy comes from the fact that Shaun often fails to see the corpses rising from the dead and is completely oblivious to the fact that they are walking along the street next to him once he works out that the world is under attack, Shaun has to try and save his family and friends from being bitten and changed into zombies

---

Resource sheet – Capital letters and full stops

Film review

Below is the article from the Activity sheet, 'A full stop confusion', with all of the full stops and capital letters in place.

Film Review
Shaun of the Dead

Released in 2004, *Shaun of the Dead* is a comedy film written by Simon Pegg and Edgar Wright. Both writers previously worked on the successful television show *Spaced*. *Shaun of the Dead* has been successful in both the UK and America. The film is about Shaun, a young man who has lots of relationship problems:

his girlfriend has just dumped him and he has arguments with his mum about his stepdad. As well as Shaun's personal problems, it seems that London, and the rest of the world, is being taken over by zombies. However, part of the comedy comes from the fact that Shaun often fails to see the corpses rising from the dead and is completely oblivious to the fact that they are walking along the street next to him. Once he works out that the world is under attack, Shaun has to try and save his family and friends from being bitten and changed into zombies.

Teacher's notes

Compound sentences

Objectives

- To understand what a compound sentence is
- To understand why compound sentences are used
- To use compound sentences within writing

Prior knowledge

It would be useful for students to have some knowledge of simple sentences and verbs.

English Framework links

Yr7 Sentence 11; Yr8 Sentence 2

Scottish attainment targets

English Language – Writing
Strand – Punctuation and structure: Level B

National Curriculum in Wales links

Writing: 3; Language development 2

Northern Ireland PoS

Language and literacy: developing their knowledge of how language works.

Background

In order for students' writing to be interesting, they need to be able to vary their sentence constructions. Students should be aware of clauses as they are writing. Once students recognise that their sentences contain clauses, they can then start to vary the sentence construction. For example, students could use a conjunction between clauses, or the more advanced student could use a subordinate clause with a main clause. This section serves as an introduction to help students understand clauses and how conjunctions can hold two clauses together.

Starter activity

The students could be given the following clauses and asked to expand them by using another verb:

- I went shopping.
- I went to the cinema.

Resource sheets and Activity sheets

So that students can start to identify compound sentences within text, they should use the Activity sheet, ' 'And', 'or' and 'but', '. This contains a number of compound sentences using common conjunctions. Students could identify these sentence types by looking out for the conjunctions. This will not only show how compound sentences are constructed but will also encourage students to adopt the use of conjunctions in their own work.

The Activity sheet, 'Write your own compound sentences', further emphasises the use of common conjunctions by asking students to insert a conjunction between two clauses. This activity will allow them to see the differences between the conjunctions, for example, how the conjunction 'or' allows an alternative piece of information to be added.

So that students fully understand the construction of a compound sentence (a clause + a conjunction + a clause) the Activity sheet, 'Time travel', shows compound sentences that have been broken down into their two clauses. Students must match the two clauses using a conjunction. The answers are: 1c; 2b; 3a; 4d.

Once students have understood the components of compound sentences, they could then start to think about why it is they are used within writing. The Activity sheet, 'Why use compound sentences?', highlights the need for a variety of sentence constructions to be used.

Finally, the Activity sheet, 'A revision of compound sentences', provides a quick activity to recap the theory learned and emphasises the need for conjunctions within students' writing.

Plenary

Referring back to the Starter activity, students could check to see if they had produced their own compound sentences; if not, they now have the knowledge to do so.

Functional English: writing © Folens

Activity sheet – Compound sentences

Time travel

☞ To complete the compound sentences below, draw an arrow from the first clause to a conjunction and then from the conjunction to the second clause. The first one has been done for you.

First clause	Conjunction	Second clause
1 For many years, people have wondered if time travel is possible…	…and…	a …the television programme *Doctor Who* is based around one man's travels in such a machine.
2 People believe that if we were to time travel, we would have to be able to travel faster than the speed of light…		b …even be able to travel through a wormhole.
3 People have long debated the idea of time machines…	…or…	c …some sceptics believe it is only possible in fiction.
4 Many filmmakers have also used time travel for the subject of their films…	…but…	d …such films have been very popular.

Activity sheet – Compound sentences

Why use compound sentences?

☞ 1 Read the extract below. The writer has not used any compound sentences. What effect does this have on his writing?

With more and more people signing up to become space tourists, the US Government has drafted up rules for anyone who wants to go into space. All space tourists must be screened. No terrorists will be allowed to fly. Nobody will be allowed to use the spacecraft as a weapon. All passengers must be healthy. Everybody will have to undergo security checks. Anyone who is banned from flying will not be allowed to fly in space. Everyone should have pre-flight training. Everyone must have knowledge of handling emergency situations.

☞ 2 Try to rewrite this paragraph in the space below using compound sentences. (Remember to use conjunctions.)

Activity sheet – Compound sentences

A revision of compound sentences

☞ Read the following passage and circle all of the conjunctions.

Anyone who wants to be an astronaut is required to have undergone aircraft training and will need to have studied some form of engineering.

All applicants should have a scientific background or science-related job experience.

To become a pilot astronaut you must have a degree in engineering or science, but a Masters degree is not always essential.

Astronauts must have completed 1000 hours of flying time in a jet aircraft and preferably had experience as a test pilot.

Physically, all applicants must pass a strict medical examination, have perfect vision and their blood pressure must be a healthy reading. They must also be between 64 inches and 76 inches tall.

Teacher's notes

Question marks

Objectives

- To understand how to use question marks
- To understand how to use question marks within dialogue

Prior knowledge

It would be useful if students understood the main rules of using dialogue within writing.

English Framework links

Yr7 Sentence 3; Yr8 Sentence 3; Yr9 Sentence 2, 4

Scottish attainment targets

English Language – Writing
Strand – Punctuation and structure: Levels C, D, E

National Curriculum in Wales links

Writing: 2; Skills 4

Northern Ireland PoS

Language and literacy: developing their knowledge of how language works.

Background

Students usually grasp the concept of question marks easily and do not seem to have any problem when understanding why they are used within writing. However, some students forget the grammatical rules behind this piece of punctuation, such as placing it within speech marks or following it with a capital letter. This section offers activities which could help to reinforce these grammatical ideas and hopefully improve students' use of the question mark.

Starter activity

Students could attempt to solve the riddle on the Resource sheet, 'Who am I?'. This will help to introduce the topic to them and expand their knowledge of question marks.

Resource sheets and Activity sheets

The Activity sheet, 'Correcting sentences', provides students with the opportunity to insert question marks where appropriate. There are several sentences that do not require question marks and it is important that students understand the principle that question marks are only required when there is a direct question.

The Activity sheet, 'Question marks and capital letters', then provides students with an activity to identify both question marks and capital letters. It is important that students understand that a question mark replaces a full stop and so should be preceded by a capital letter. The Resource sheet, 'The answers', provides students with a corrected version of the previous task so that they can check their own answers.

The Activity sheet, 'Using question marks within dialogue', shows students how to use this piece of punctuation when using speech marks. This helps to enforce the position of the question mark within speech marks.

Plenary

Students could be asked to compile a list of five sentences, some of which will require a question mark and some which will not. The students should hand this list to another student who should insert the correct punctuation.

Functional English: writing

Who am I?

I am a piece of punctuation.

I can replace a full stop.

I am used at the end of a sentence.

I am usually followed by a capital letter.

In some foreign languages, such as Spanish, I am turned upside down.

I am sometimes used in cartoons in a speech bubble over a character's head to show that they are confused.

I appear on the Riddler's costume in the film, *Batman Forever*.

I have a dot at the bottom.

Correcting sentences

☞ Read the following sentences and put either a question mark or a full stop at the end of each one.

- He should go to the staffroom, shouldn't he

- They're settling in well, aren't they

- Are you ok

- The teacher asked the girl what she was doing

- Do you think they will sell it there

- I wonder if they will sell it

- I'll ask my sister about her car

- Shall I ask my sister about her car

- Should we finish now

- Did you see that film last week

- Ask her about the film

- Did he use to live there

- I asked him whether he once lived there

Question marks and capital letters

☞ The following text is missing question marks and capital letters. Write in where you think the question marks should go and circle the letters you think should be in capitals.

Do you know how many phobias there are it seems that the world is full of strange fears with weird and wonderful names these days so we've decided to take a look at some of these common phobias.

Have you ever been frightened by thunder and lightning if so, you may be suffering from the common phobia, brontophobia. It is a fear that many young children suffer from but it usually disappears when you reach adulthood.

Do you suffer from this one when you go on your holidays aerophobia is the fear of flying, whether it is fear of flying in a plane, jet or hot-air balloon.

This next phobia causes problems for people when they are getting dressed. It is chromophobia. Have you heard of it it is a fear of colours. How would you cope with your day-to-day activities if you were frightened of colours

It seems that in this modern world, people can be frightened of almost anything. However, where there's a fear, there's generally a cure of some sort. We only need to worry when we learn that there's a fear of cures!

Resource sheet – Question marks

The answers

Below is the text from the Activity sheet, 'Question marks and capital letters', with all of the question marks and capital letters in place – see if you got them all right!

Do you know how many phobias there are? It seems that the world is full of strange fears with weird and wonderful names these days so we've decided to take a look at some of these common phobias.

Have you ever been frightened by thunder and lightning? If so, you may be suffering from the common phobia, brontophobia. It is a fear that many young children suffer from but it usually disappears when you reach adulthood.

Do you suffer from this one when you go on your holidays? Aerophobia is the fear of flying, whether it is fear of flying in a plane, jet or hot-air balloon.

This next phobia causes problems for people when they are getting dressed. It is chromophobia. Have you heard of it? It is a fear of colours. How would you cope with your day-to-day activities if you were frightened of colours?

It seems that in this modern world, people can be frightened of almost anything. However, where there's a fear, there's generally a cure of some sort. We only need to worry when we learn that there's a fear of cures!

Activity sheet – Question marks

Using question marks within dialogue

At the end of dialogue, before the closing speech marks, there should always be a piece of punctuation.

 Have a look at the text below – it is missing punctuation before the closing speech marks. Insert all of the correct pieces of punctuation in the spaces provided.

"Please sir, would you mind storing that bag in the overhead locker ____" the air stewardess asked politely.

"Yes, I would mind. It's got valuable equipment inside ____" grumbled the businessman, as he read his newspaper.

"Sir, the regulations state that all hand luggage must go into the locker for security reasons. It will only be for take-off. Now, should I put it up there for you ____" the stewardess said, with a slightly annoyed tone.

"You're no doubt going to do it anyway, aren't you? Go on then, but if anything happens to it, I'll be asking you to pay for the damage ____" he said, in a louder, more irritable tone.

"Certainly sir. Please enjoy your flight ____" the stewardess said, through gritted teeth.

Teacher's notes

Plan, draft and organise

Objectives

- To understand the importance of planning
- To understand the importance of drafting and redrafting
- To understand how to organise texts effectively

Prior knowledge

Students should have knowledge of a previous writing or exam task that has required them to undertake planning or drafting.

English Framework links

Yr7 Sentence 12; Yr8 Sentence 6; Yr9 Sentence 5

Scottish attainment targets

English Language – Writing
Strand – Functional writing: Levels A, B, C, D, E

National Curriculum in Wales links

Writing: 2; Skills 1

Northern Ireland PoS

Language and literacy: developing an understanding of different forms.

Background

Planning and drafting are important stages of the writing process and students should understand how authorial craft can be altered and improved by effective planning and drafting.

Starter activity

In order to emphasise the importance of the planning stage when creating a text, students could complete the Activity sheet, 'The planning stages'. This sheet focuses on the main essential stages of effective planning, from reading a question to writing a text. The sheet contains correct and incorrect advice about planning. Students should identify the tips which are correct and those which are incorrect.

Resource sheets and Activity sheets

The Activity sheet, 'Which comes first?', explores the order of the planning stages that students should follow when completing a task. They should read each of the stages and try to reorganise them into the correct order. These tips focus upon the basic elements of planning, such as underlining keywords in a question, rereading the question and planning the content of each paragraph. The correct order is: 5; 3; 1; 6; 2; 4.

The Resource sheet, 'How to plan', shows students how to put their planning skills into practise by using an example. This sheet shows an example of a student's initial planning and notes made before attempting to answer a question. The sheet guides students through the important areas to consider when attempting to create a text.

The Activity sheet, 'Organising your letter writing', gives the suggested content of each paragraph of a letter, however, they are not in the correct order. Students need to try and organise the boxes into the correct order.

Plenary

Students should attempt to create their own plan by completing the Activity sheet, 'Writing a plan'. They should imagine that they need to plan ideas for a letter; they need to think about their initial ideas for the audience, content, style and structure of their writing. This task helps to revise the main elements of the planning stages.

Activity sheet – Plan, draft and organise

The planning stages

When you are faced with a writing task, it is important that you plan your answer before you begin.

☞ This page contains lots of advice about planning a piece of writing, but only five of them contain correct advice. Put a tick next to the ones that are correct and a cross next to the ones that are incorrect.

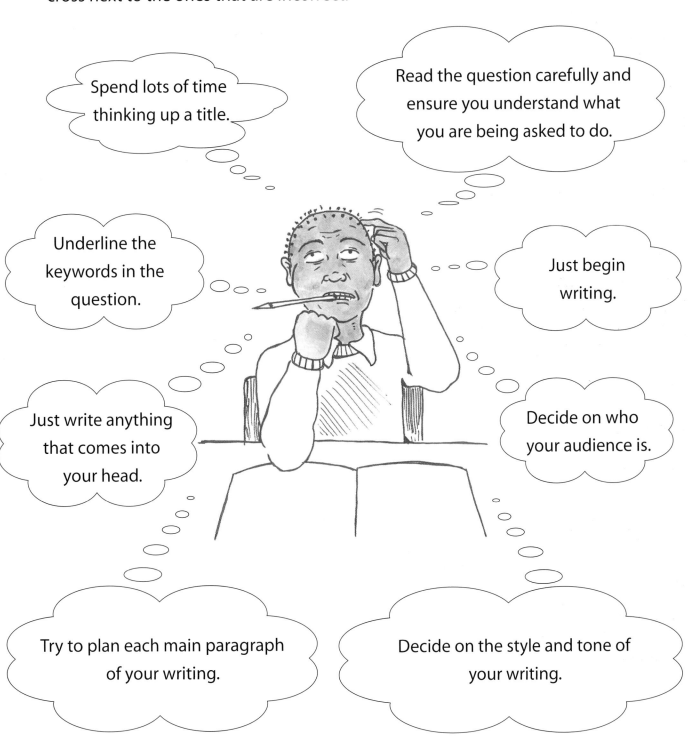

Spend lots of time thinking up a title.

Read the question carefully and ensure you understand what you are being asked to do.

Underline the keywords in the question.

Just begin writing.

Just write anything that comes into your head.

Decide on who your audience is.

Try to plan each main paragraph of your writing.

Decide on the style and tone of your writing.

Activity sheet – Plan, draft and organise

Which comes first?

☞ The following list contains important stages of the planning and drafting process. Try to rewrite them in the spaces below so that the stages are in the correct order.

1   Decide on who your audience is.

2   Try to plan each main paragraph of your writing.

3   Underline the keywords in the question.

4   Reread your work and check that you have done what you were asked to do.

5   Read the question carefully and ensure you understand what you are being asked to do.

6   Decide on the style and tone of your writing.

The correct planning order should be:

1   _____

_____

2   _____

_____

3   _____

_____

4   _____

_____

5   _____

_____

6   _____

_____

Resource sheet – Plan, draft and organise

How to plan

A student has been asked to write a letter to their head teacher, asking if they could organise a non-uniform day for charity.

The boxes below will give you some ideas about what the student is thinking about while preparing their letter.

What is the main topic? ● To ask if a non-uniform day at school can be organised for charity.	**Who is your audience?** ● The head teacher.
What is the writing style/layout? ● It must be a letter so needs to include 'Dear (head teacher's name)' and 'Yours sincerely', because the letter is being addressed to someone whose name is known.	**What are the main points?** ● Introduce the main topic and explain which charity is to be supported and why. ● Explain how the idea would work. ● Thank the head teacher for reading the letter.
What structure should be used? ● Use paragraphs.	**Is there anything else I should think about?** ● Need to use formal language. ● Must be polite.

Activity sheet – Plan, draft and organise

Organising your letter writing

Below are some ideas on how you should prepare each paragraph of a letter, however, they are all jumbled up.

☞ Read through all of the paragraphs and try to decide in which order they should be in. Write 1 to 5 in the spaces provided to indicate the correct order.

Paragraph number _____

This paragraph must explain your first idea, or first point, in detail. If you need to, you should support each point and ensure they are explained properly.

You could begin this paragraph with the word 'firstly'.

Paragraph number _____

This paragraph should go on to explain your second main point or idea. Again, this must be detailed and your idea must be easy to understand and clear to your audience.

You may wish to begin this paragraph with the word 'secondly'.

Paragraph number _____

This paragraph must reach a conclusion. You may wish to summarise your main ideas and thank the reader for taking the time to read your letter.

You may wish to begin this paragraph with the word 'finally'.

Paragraph number _____

This paragraph would be an introduction to your letter. It must introduce the main point or idea behind your writing. It must set the tone and style for the rest of the letter.

Paragraph number _____

This paragraph will explain your third main idea or point. It should also be detailed.

Activity sheet – Plan, draft and organise

Writing a plan

You have been asked to write a letter to your local council, asking them to build a leisure centre in your area for young people to use.

☞ 1 Write some ideas down in the boxes below to help you prepare your letter.

What is the main topic?	Who is your audience?
What is the writing style/layout?	**What are the main points?**
What structure should be used?	**Is there anything else I should think about?**

☞ 2 Using your notes, write out the letter in your work book.

Teacher's notes

Verb tense and subject verb agreement

Objectives

- To understand the use of verbs
- To understand the use of tenses
- To understand the importance of consistency in the use of verbs and tenses
- To understand the importance of subject verb agreement

Prior knowledge

Students should have knowledge of using verbs and tenses. They should also have a basic understanding of the role of verbs and tenses.

English Framework links

Yr7 Sentence 4; Yr8 Sentence 4

Scottish attainment targets

English Language – Writing
Strand – Knowledge and language: Level C

National Curriculum in Wales links

Writing: 3; Language development 2

Northern Ireland PoS

Language and literacy: developing their knowledge of how language works.

Background

One common error made by many students is using a mixture of tenses throughout a piece of writing. Errors are also often made in the use of subject verb agreements. By ensuring students understand the basic rules of these grammatical areas and by practising these skills, their writing can be greatly improved.

Starter activity

Students can begin by testing their knowledge of verbs and subject verb agreements. They should think of three verbs and for each verb, try to write two sentences using them with a different tense. This task encourages students to think about their use of different tenses, as well as focusing their attention on their verb endings.

Resource sheets and Activity sheets

The Resource sheet, 'Verbs and tenses', provides students with a clear definition of a verb and a tense. Students could use this sheet for reference throughout the tasks that follow.

The Activity sheet, 'Verbs, verbs, verbs', tests students' ability to select and highlight the verbs used within text. Students should also see if they can decide which tense is being used in each example.

The Activity sheet, 'Using verbs to create a tense', explains how a verb should be adapted to create the tense of a piece of writing. The table on the sheet contains sentences written in both past and present tense. Students should try to complete the gaps in the table, changing the tense of the sentences to ensure the verb endings are correct.

By reading the text on the Activity sheet, 'Present tense verbs', students are given a clear example as to how the present tense is constructed. The students should try to complete the tasks on this sheet including writing their own text, using the past tense. As they complete this activity, their attention should be drawn to the importance of ensuring their verb endings are correct for the tense and that they should concentrate on their subject verb agreement. This activity can be supported by using the Resource sheet, 'Subject verb agreement', which provides students with a clear definition of the subject of a sentence. Those struggling to understand this area should try to underline the subject within the key sentences on this sheet. The table on this sheet also shows students an example of how the ending of their verb can change, depending upon the subject and the tense.

Plenary

Students should look again at the table on the Resource sheet, 'Subject verb agreement', and try to write their own table for two other verbs. They should concentrate on using the correct verb endings in each case.

Resource sheet – Verb tense and subject verb agreement

Verbs and tenses

A verb is an action or 'doing' word. For example:

- I <u>cry</u> at sad films.
- I always <u>eat</u> breakfast.
- I also go to <u>sleep</u> really quickly.
- I <u>laugh</u> at my friends' jokes.
- I sometimes <u>walk</u> to school.

The tense used in a piece of writing tells the reader whether the events took place in the past, the present or will take place in the future. For example:

Past	Present	Future
I <u>cried</u> last night.	I am <u>crying</u> at the film.	I will probably <u>cry</u> tomorrow because I am going to watch another sad film.
I <u>ate</u> a really nice meal yesterday.	I am <u>eating</u> my lunch.	I am going to <u>eat</u> chips later.
I <u>walked</u> to the shop.	I am <u>walking</u> to the shop.	I will <u>walk</u> to the shops after school.

Activity sheet – Verb tense and subject verb agreement

Verbs, verbs, verbs

☞ 1 Read the following paragraphs and try to underline all of the verbs.

My friends and I have decided to watch some films later tonight. On the way home from school we are going to buy some popcorn and order a pizza afterwards. One of the films looks like it is going to really be sad so I think some people might cry. The other one is a comedy, which I think will make everyone laugh.

I walked to the shop, even though it was raining. It was freezing so I pulled my coat collar up to stop the pouring rain trickling down my neck. The cars moved slowly in the rush hour traffic and some drivers beeped their horns angrily. As I reached the end of the road, a taxi rushed passed me, splashing muddy water from the gutter all over my jeans. I groaned and shivered.

I have just realised that I've forgotten to do my homework so I am writing it on the bus to school. I can't remember what the answers are to some of the history questions so I think I will ask my friends as soon as they get picked up.

☞ 2 Can you tell which tense is being used in each paragraph?

Activity sheet – Verb tense and subject verb agreement

Using verbs to create a tense

It is important that you use the correct tense all the way through your writing. You must make sure that you use the correct verb endings to do this.

☞ The following table contains different sentences which use verbs. Try and complete the gaps in the table by deciding how the sentence and the verb should be written to create either a past or present tense. The first one has been done for you.

Past tense	Present tense
I ate my dinner.	I am eating my dinner.
	I am baking a cake.
I sent the letter yesterday.	
	I am playing a game.
	I am walking to school.
We slept in a tent.	
	I can't stop laughing.
I cried when I watched the film.	
	I am writing a story.
I ran across the road.	

Activity sheet – Verb tense and subject verb agreement

Present tense verbs

☞ 1 The following paragraph has been written in the present tense. Read the text and then underline three sentences which use a verb in the present tense.

I hate Maths so I am skipping the lesson. It's my worst subject. The teacher drives me mad. She doesn't like me and I don't like her. Every week I tell her I have forgotten my homework and we both know it is a lie; I just don't do my homework. It's not that I want to be awkward, it's just that I can't do Maths, it's too difficult. I think there is a part of my brain missing – the Maths part. The part that everyone else gets given at birth is missing. So every week I skip the lesson. I sit in the toilets, bored.

☞ 2 The narrator is now an adult and is looking back on their schooldays. In the space below try to rewrite the paragraph from the point of view of the narrator now they are older. Remember to check that you are using the correct tense and verb endings throughout.

Resource sheet – Verb tense and subject verb agreement

Subject verb agreement

A subject is the character involved in, or doing, the action. For example:

- I ate the piece of cake.

  'I' is the subject because the character is eating the cake.

- Tom ran across the road.

  'Tom' is the subject because he is the character who is running.

- Harry threw his bag onto the floor.

  'Harry' is the subject because he is the character who threw the bag.

- We go to the cinema every Saturday.

  'We' is the subject because the characters are going to the cinema.

- They dribbled the football around the playground.

  'They' is the subject because the characters are dribbling the football.

The following examples combine a subject and a verb in the past and present tense:

Past tense	Present tense
• I walked	• I walk
• You walked	• You walk
• He/she walked	• He/she walks
• They walked	• They walk
• We walked	• We walk

Teacher's notes

Logical sequencing

Objectives

- To understand the importance of an effective structure
- To understand how to create a logical sequence and order within a text

Prior knowledge

Students should have prior knowledge of writing a text which required a logical sequence or order.

English Framework links

Yr7 Sentence 8, 10, 12; Yr8 Sentence 6, 7; Yr9 Sentence 5, 6

Scottish attainment targets

English Language – Writing
Strand – Punctuation and structure: Levels C, D, E

National Curriculum in Wales links

Writing: 3; Language development 2

Northern Ireland PoS

Language and literacy: developing an understanding of different forms, genres and methods of communication.

Background

Many students forget to concentrate on the structuring of their work and lose marks as a result. It is important to remind students that using structure and sequence within their writing is a valuable authorial technique and something which should be considered throughout the planning, writing and redrafting processes.

Starter activity

A useful Starter activity would be to ask students to read the text on the Activity sheet, 'Which order?'. This piece of description focuses upon a strange event that happened to the narrator one evening; however, the paragraphs have been jumbled up. Students should try to rearrange the paragraphs into the correct order so that the text makes more sense. Once they have completed this activity, the students should discuss how they came to their final decision. Their attention should be drawn to the sequencing techniques and clues used by the writer.

Resource sheets and Activity sheets

Students could try to write their own short description about a strange event that may have happened to them and aim to write three paragraphs. The important factor is that their paragraphs should use sequencing devices to indicate a logical order for the reader. Students could use the Resource sheet, 'Sequencing devices', to help them. This sheet lists possible words and phrases they could use to help indicate sequence within their work.

The Activity sheet, 'Using a clear sequence', tests the students' knowledge of sequencing devices. This informative text uses several devices which help to sequence the text. Students should try to underline all of the words and phrases which help the writer to achieve a logical structure.

Students can then try to apply the words and phrases they have learned to the Activity sheet, 'Making a cup of coffee'. This asks them to imagine that they have to explain to an alien how to make a cup of coffee. The sheet gives brief, illustrated points of the main stages in making a drink, but these need to be rewritten in continuous prose. The students should use words and phrases to create a clear and logical sequence in their written instructions. They should be reminded of the importance of the text being as straightforward and clear for the reader as possible.

Plenary

Students could complete the task on the Activity sheet, 'Where am I going?'. This asks them to write a set of directions for another student. Students should be reminded of the need for their writing to be as clear and as straightforward as possible. One way in which they can achieve this is to ensure they are using appropriate words and phrases which indicate sequence and order. Their skills could be put to the test to see if their directions really work!

Activity sheet – Logical sequencing

Which order?

It is important that your writing follows a clear and logical order. Each idea must follow on from the other so that the reader is able to follow your ideas easily.

☞ The following piece of writing is jumbled up. Can you try to decide which order the paragraphs should be in so that the text makes more sense? Write 1 against the paragraph you think should be first, write 2 against the second paragraph, and so on.

Mum slowly opened the front door, still leaving the safety catch on. I stood in the doorway of the lounge, peering over her shoulder trying to see who it was. As she gradually opened the door a little wider, it became clear that there was nobody there.

As I said, Mum was about to go for her bath and just as she was about to climb the stairs, the doorbell rang. This surprised us both as we don't normally get visitors on a week night, especially not at that time. Mum hates having to answer the door at night.

It was last Tuesday night when it happened. I think it was probably about eight o'clock, because I remember that we had just watched *Coronation Street* and Mum was about to go for her bath. I can't believe a week has passed since then. It seems like only yesterday.

After calling out 'Hello?' several times, Mum finally took the safety catch off the door and angrily opened the door wider, peering into the dark, cold night. The wind whistled through the house and Mum cursed angrily as the cat made a bid for freedom, running down the driveway into the darkness.

Sequencing devices

The following bullet points outline some words and phrases you could use when beginning your writing, introducing additional ideas and then ending your writing.

Words and phrases to begin your writing:

- Firstly
- One day
- To begin with
- The first idea
- It was Tuesday night when

Words and phrases to introduce additional ideas and points:

- Also
- A further idea
- Another thing that happened was
- As well as

Words and phrases to end your writing:

- In conclusion
- To conclude
- Finally
- In the end

Using a clear sequence

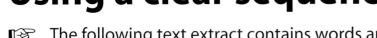

☞ The following text extract contains words and phrases which help to show a logical order to the paragraphs. Try to underline any words or phrases which you think help make the order clear for the reader.

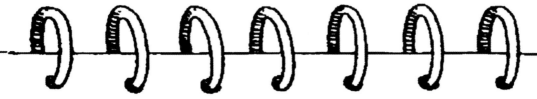

When you begin to write a story, the first thing you need to think about is your setting. It is important that you create an imaginative scene for your reader so try to think of somewhere interesting and exciting to set your story.

Secondly, you need to decide upon your main character. This character will be involved in most of the action within your story so they must be someone that the reader wants to read about. Try to think about every detail of this character and describe them clearly. The reader must be able to imagine exactly what the character looks like.

Once you have your character, another area you need to focus on is the main events that happen in your story. Every good story has some sort of event as this is the part which keeps the reader interested; you want to make them read on. Perhaps something will happen to your main character? Or maybe there will be a problem that they have to solve?

Finally, you need a good ending. Don't rush the end of your story, or your reader will be disappointed. The ending could shock or surprise them or it may solve any problems that the character has encountered throughout the story.

Activity sheet – Logical sequencing

Making a cup of coffee

Aliens have landed on earth and they have no idea how to carry out everyday tasks. You will need to try and explain to them how to make themselves a cup of coffee!

☞ Below are some simple instructions which you will need to change into more detailed paragraphs, making each stage as clear as possible. Make sure that you use words and phrases which indicate a logical sequence so that the aliens know which order to do everything in.

Fill kettle and switch on

Put coffee and milk in mug

Add hot water from kettle and stir

Drink

　　　Functional English: writing　　　© Folens (copiable page)

Activity sheet – Logical sequencing

Where am I going?

Using your sequencing skills, you are going to try and direct one of your friends around your school.

When giving directions to other people it is important that you use words and phrases which create a logical order. Your reader will need to be able to follow your instructions step-by-step, otherwise they will get lost!

☞ 1 Decide on a starting point and an end point in your school. Use the space below to try and write a set of clear directions. You could use words and phrases from the following list to help you:

- Thirdly
- Once you have
- Firstly
- Finally
- The next step
- Secondly
- Also

☞ 2 Once you have written your directions, get a friend to try and follow them and see if they end up in the correct place.

Teacher's notes

Complex sentences

Objectives

- To understand sentence structures
- To understand how to vary sentence structures
- Be able to recognise varying sentence structures

Prior knowledge

Students should have the ability to recognise simple and complex sentences within a text.

English Framework links

Yr7 Sentence 1; Yr8 Sentence 1, 2; Yr9 Sentence 1

Scottish attainment targets

English Language – Writing
Strand – Knowledge about language: Level E

National Curriculum in Wales links

Writing: 3; Language development 1

Northern Ireland PoS

Language and literacy: developing their knowledge of how language works.

Background

An effective authorial technique which students can use to improve their work is to use varying sentence structures. Students should be able to recognise varying sentence structures in the work of other writers, as well as be able to use more sophisticated sentence forms to improve the quality of their own writing.

Starter activity

A quick Starter activity could be to ask the students to write a short, simple sentence which gives a piece of information about themselves. They should then be told that this sentence has to be lengthened, with more detail. The aim is for them to change their simple sentence into a complex sentence.

Resource sheets and Activity sheets

Students should be guided through the Resource sheet, 'What is a complex sentence?'. This sheet should be retained and used by the students for future revision. The sheet gives a clear definition of a complex sentence structure. Students should be made aware of the structure of the two clauses within a complex sentence. Students could be asked to discuss reasons why a writer would choose to use a complex sentence over a simple sentence and the impact complex sentences can have upon a text.

Students' understanding of complex sentences can be tested using the Activity sheet, 'Recognising complex sentences'. It is important that as well as being able to write their own complex sentences, students are able to recognise the structures used by other writers. This sheet asks students to read a piece of text and underline any complex sentences that have been used by the writer.

The Activity sheet, 'Complex or not?', requires students to assess some sentences. The table contains a list of sentences, of which some are simple and some are complex; students must decide which they are. They should be encouraged to support their decisions, giving reasons for their answer and try to analyse the writer's use of main and subordinate clauses. This can be taken further using the Activity sheet, 'Main or subordinate?', which encourages students to further analyse the structure of complex sentences.

Plenary

Students should try to complete the task on the Activity sheet, 'Using complex sentences'. This shows a piece of text that uses very few complex sentences. Students should try to improve the text by adding some of their own complex sentences, or by trying to expand upon the writer's simple sentences by adding more detail. Their attention should be drawn to the fact that an entire text should not be made up of just complex sentences, but that by varying their sentence structures, a writer can produce a more imaginative and interesting piece of work.

Resource sheet – Complex sentences

What is a complex sentence?

Complex sentences usually have at least one main clause plus a subordinate clause.
For example:

I went shopping even though it was raining.

The **main clause** is the main point of the conversation, meaning that the sentence would make sense on its own, even if there wasn't a subordinate clause.

In this example, 'I went shopping', would make sense on its own as a sentence.

The **subordinate clause** will not make sense on its own and can go either before or after the main clause.

In this example, 'even though it was raining', would not make sense as a sentence on its own.

Here are some more examples:

I bought a new top even though I had no money.

Main clause	Subordinate clause
'I bought a new top'	'even though I had no money'

I'm going to the cinema with some friends tonight.

Main clause	Subordinate clause
'I'm going to the cinema'	'with some friends tonight'

Activity sheet – Complex sentences

Recognising complex sentences

A complex sentence:

- is usually longer than a simple sentence

- will give more than one piece of information

- will include a main clause (the main point of the sentence) and a subordinate clause (which adds extra information).

☞ Read the following paragraphs and try to underline any complex sentences.

Even though I wasn't hungry, I ate my sandwich. It gave me something to do. I was bored. I had never been so bored in my whole life. Lunch time was a few hours away but I couldn't concentrate any longer. Eating helped to stop the boredom. If only I had something interesting to do. But I didn't.

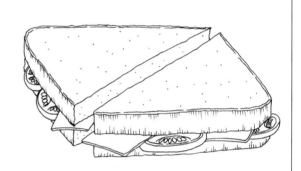

I shivered, even though it was a hot day. I felt funny. I was nervous. The day seemed to have gone on forever but it was only lunchtime. My driving test wasn't far away now. Only four hours left. I wish it was sooner. I just wanted to get it over and done with.

The exam was in a few hours but I knew I wouldn't be able to concentrate. I was too nervous. I wish I had studied more. The weather had just been so sunny. It would have been a shame to stay locked up indoors. Wish I had though!

Activity sheet – Complex sentences

Complex or not?

The following table contains different sentences. Some of them are complex and some of them are not.

☞   In the table below put a tick next to any complex sentences and a cross next to any simple sentences. The first one has been done for you.

Sentence	Is it complex?
I hate Maths.	✗
I like English even though it is sometimes difficult.	
Despite trying hard, I failed the exam.	
The lady ate her sandwich, even though she was not hungry.	
The dark room was cold.	
The cat ran out.	
I love animals but I am allergic to them.	
The sun shone brightly.	
Screaming loudly, I ran out of the room.	
I was hungry.	
I couldn't wait to go on holiday this Saturday.	
The snow started falling.	
I have homework.	

Activity sheet – Complex sentences

Main or subordinate?

☞ Read the following complex sentences and try to identify the main clause and the subordinate clause in each one by writing them in the boxes provided.

● My car was broken into whilst I was in the café.

Main clause:	Subordinate clause:

● The train picked up speed, helping the driver to gain time.

Main clause:	Subordinate clause:

● I hate chicken because the smell makes me feel sick.

Main clause:	Subordinate clause:

● Despite wearing my raincoat, I was soaked to the bone.

Main clause:	Subordinate clause:

● He was angry, despite it being his birthday.

Main clause:	Subordinate clause:

Activity sheet – Complex sentences

Using complex sentences

The following piece of descriptive text contains only a few complex sentences.

 Read the extract below and then try to rewrite it in the space provided, adding complex sentences to make it more interesting.

I didn't expect to be there for so long. The clock ticked loudly. I waited for them in the reception area. I could hear their voices through the door. He kept shouting. She stayed calm throughout the whole meeting.

I tapped my feet. My stomach churned. I knew I was going to be in trouble. Why had I done it? What was I going to tell her? She was going to go mad. I knew she would be disappointed in me.

I felt terrible. I had promised not to do this again. I had let her down. She was going to be so upset. I needed to plan my story now. I knew I wouldn't know what to say to her. I tried to plan the words in my head.

Teacher's notes

Apostrophes

Objectives

- To understand the role of apostrophes
- To understand the rules of using apostrophes

Prior knowledge

Students should have previously used or can recognise the use of apostrophes within writing.

English Framework links

Yr7 Sentence 3; Yr8 Sentence 3; Yr9 Sentence 2

Scottish attainment targets

English Language – Writing
Strand – Punctuation and structure: Levels C, D, E

National Curriculum in Wales links

Writing: 2; Skills 4

Northern Ireland PoS

Language and literacy: developing their knowledge of how language works.

Background

Apostrophes are a form of punctuation which students often find the most difficult. Many become overwhelmed by their various uses and rules. By working through the activities, students' confidence should increase, allowing them to use apostrophes for varying purposes throughout their own writing.

Starter activity

The Activity sheet, 'How much do you know?', is a suitable starter activity to assess the students' current knowledge of apostrophes. This sheet contains a list of sentences, all missing an apostrophe. Students should try to decide where the apostrophe should be placed.

Once this unit has been completed, students can return to these initial answers and see how many they got correct.

Resource sheets and Activity sheets

The Activity sheet, 'Apostrophes for ownership', focuses upon one of the most common areas where students fail to use apostrophes. This sheet provides a clear explanation of the use of apostrophes for ownership and students should retain this for future reference. Students should try to complete the activity, inserting the apostrophes in the correct places.

The Activity sheet, 'Apostrophes for omission', looks at the second use of apostrophes. Again, this sheet provides a clear explanation of the use of apostrophes in this case and students should retain this definition for future reference. Students should complete the table on the sheet, writing the shortened version of each word, using an apostrophe for omission. They should be reminded that such shortened words are not appropriate for all writing styles and that in more formal writing, the full version of the words should be used.

Many students become confused when using apostrophes within plurals. The Activity sheet, 'Apostrophes and plurals', explains the basic rules of using apostrophes for plurals and gives a short activity for students to test their understanding.

Plenary

Students should try to complete the task on the Activity sheet, 'Testing your knowledge', which consolidates all they have covered on apostrophes. The task requires them to rewrite a text and insert the missing apostrophes. The text requires both apostrophes for possession and apostrophes with plurals. There are also several words which can be shortened, using apostrophes for omission.

Activity sheet – Apostrophes

How much do you know?

☞ Each of the following sentences needs to have an apostrophe. Read each one and try to rewrite them, remembering to insert an apostrophe in the correct place.

- **The ladys bag was battered and old.**

- **The boys books were all soaking wet from the rain.**

- **I threw Susans book across the room.**

- **Shes the best teacher in the school.**

- **Its too hot today.**

- **I like him; hes very funny.**

Apostrophes for ownership

Apostrophes can be used to show the ownership of something. For example:

The boy's books.

As the books all belong to only one person (the boy), the apostrophe and the 's' together indicates this to the reader.

All of the sentences below need to show ownership. At the moment they do not make sense.

☞ See if you can rewrite the sentences, remembering to include an apostrophe and an 's' in the correct place.

- **Jo shoes were new.**

- **Mary bag was stolen.**

- **The cat dinner was in a saucer on the kitchen floor.**

- **Kayleigh ferret needed a wash.**

- **John PE bag had gone missing.**

- **Daniel last minute goal won the football match for his team.**

- **Cathy work was almost finished.**

- **The girl computer crashed and she lost all of her work.**

Activity sheet – Apostrophes

Apostrophes for omission

Apostrophes can be used to shorten words or replace missing letters. This is called 'omission'. For example:

I don<u>'</u>t want to go to the cinema.

If this sentence was written in its full form, it would read:

I <u>do not</u> want to go to the cinema.

The words 'do not' can be shortened to make the word 'don't' by replacing the missing letters with an apostrophe.

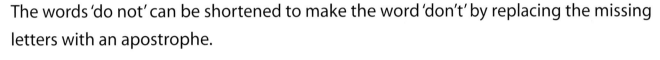 There are lots of words that can be shortened by using an apostrophe. The following table contains examples of these words. See if you can write the shortened version in the table below, using apostrophes.

Full form	Shortened version
would not	
could not	
should not	
do not	
can not	
have not	

Apostrophes and plurals

A plural shows that there is more than one of something. If you want to show that there is more than one object, you would add an 's' onto the end of the word.

For example, if you have more than one book, the word would become:

book<u>s</u>

Plurals become tricky when you need to imply ownership as well. Many people find this the most difficult use for apostrophes.

It is important that you remember the basic rules of using apostrophes with plurals. For example, if you need to show that the books belong to *one* boy, you would write the plural first and then add the possessive apostrophe *before* the 's':

The boy<u>'</u>s books.

However, if you needed to show that the books belong to *more* than one boy, you would write the possessive apostrophe *after* the 's':

The boys<u>'</u> books.

☞ The following sentences use possessive apostrophes. Try to change them using plurals and apostrophes. The first one has been done for you.

The girl's bag.	The girls' bags.
The dog's kennel.	
The cat's basket.	
The boy's homework diary.	

Activity sheet – Apostrophes

Testing your knowledge

☞ All of the apostrophes are missing from the following text. Rewrite the extract in the box below, remembering to add apostrophes in the correct places. You should also try to shorten any words that could use omission apostrophes.

I was starving and I knew I should not have done it, but they were just sitting there. It was as if they were calling to me: Alans sandwiches, they looked so inviting. He had forgotten to take them to work. If I did not eat them, they would only get thrown away. I made them for him anyway, so I suppose I had the right to eat them. Perhaps he would forget they were there and never know I ate them.

As I reached inside the fridge, I made another great discovery; Chloe and Emilys chocolates! So after eating Alans sandwich, I then committed a worse crime and ate the girls food too!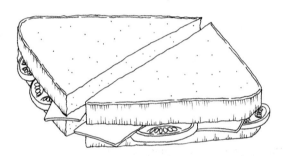

Assessment sheet – Functional English: writing

✓ Tick the boxes to show what you know or what you can do.

	Yes	Not sure	Don't know
I listen to the teacher.			
I work well with a partner.			
I can work well in a group.			
●			
●			
●			
●			
●			
●			
●			

The thing that I remember most about this unit is:

_____

_____

I need to work on (up to three targets):

1 _____

2 _____

3 _____

Functional English: writing